IN 1900 THE BROTHERS START BUILDING THEIR FIRST GLIDER IN THE BICYCLE SHOP WORKROOM, USING ODDS AND ENDS THEY FIND CLOSE AT HAND.

WRIGHT CYCLE CO.

NOT BAD FOR JUST FIFTEEN DOLLARS TOTAL!

YOU'RE RIGHT ABOUT THAT, WILBUR WRIGHT.

NOW WE BEGIN TESTING IT. BUT WHERE?

AND *HOW*?

THE FINISHED GLIDER HAS A WINGSPAN OF 17 FEET AND WEIGHS 52 POUNDS. AN AMAZING SIGHT!

USING WHAT THEY LEARNED FROM THE FLIGHT OF BIRDS, WILBUR AND ORVILLE CONSTRUCT SLIGHTLY MOVABLE, OR WARPED, WINGS.

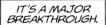

IT'S A MAJOR BREAKTHROUGH.

AT FIRST THE PILOT CONTROLS THE GLIDER'S SIDEWAYS BALANCE, OR ROLL, WITH HIS FEET. LATER HE WILL DO THIS BY ROTATING HIS HIPS.

THE PILOT IS NOW FREE TO MANAGE THE FRONT RUDDER, OR ELEVATOR, WITH HIS HANDS. THE ELEVATOR CONTROLS THE UP AND DOWN MOVEMENTS OF THE GLIDER'S NOSE.

CAN OUR DATA BE INCORRECT?

LATE INTO THE NIGHTS, AS WAVES LAP AGAINST THE NEARBY SHORE, THE BROTHERS TALK, TALK, AND TALK SOME MORE.

WE DESIGNED THE ANGLE, LENGTH, AND WEIGHT OF THE WINGS ACCORDING TO LILIENTHAL'S AIR-PRESSURE TABLES.

YES. BUT COULD THOSE TABLES BE WRONG?

BUT THEIR DREAMS WILL NOT DIE. BACK IN DAYTON, THE WRIGHTS CONTINUE TO ASK QUESTIONS.

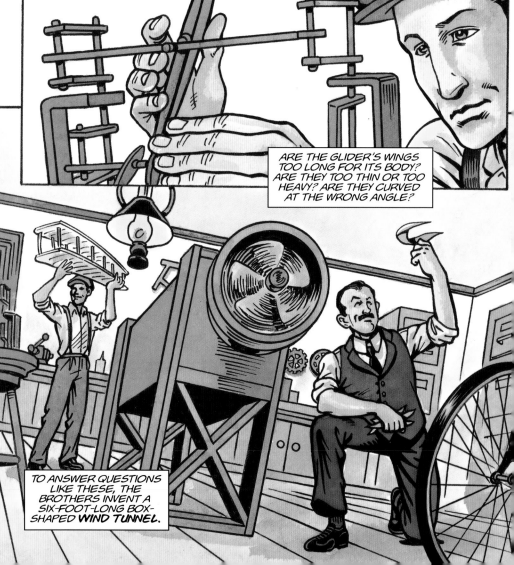

ARE THE GLIDER'S WINGS TOO LONG FOR ITS BODY? ARE THEY TOO THIN OR TOO HEAVY? ARE THEY CURVED AT THE WRONG ANGLE?

TO ANSWER QUESTIONS LIKE THESE, THE BROTHERS INVENT A SIX-FOOT-LONG BOX-SHAPED **WIND TUNNEL**.

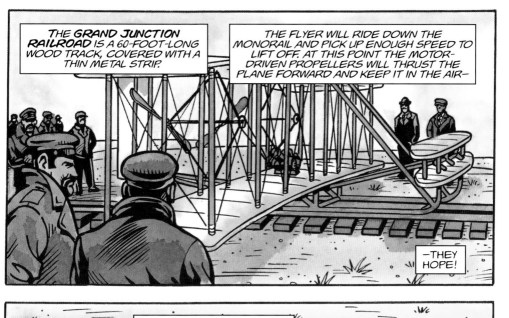

THE **GRAND JUNCTION RAILROAD** IS A 60-FOOT-LONG WOOD TRACK, COVERED WITH A THIN METAL STRIP.

THE FLYER WILL RIDE DOWN THE MONORAIL AND PICK UP ENOUGH SPEED TO LIFT OFF. AT THIS POINT THE MOTOR-DRIVEN PROPELLERS WILL THRUST THE PLANE FORWARD AND KEEP IT IN THE AIR—

—THEY HOPE!

DECEMBER 14, 1903, WILBUR AND ORVILLE FEEL THEY CAN DELAY NO LONGER.

WITH THE HELP OF MEN FROM THE LOCAL LIFE-SAVING STATION, THEY DRAG THE 600-POUND FLYER TO THE TOP OF BIG KILL DEVIL HILL.

ARE YOU TRYING TO TELL ME THAT SOMETHING THIS HEAVY IS GOING TO GET OFF THE GROUND?

GET READY TO HOLD YOUR EARS WHEN IT CRASHES!

BUT... NOT YET:

OH NO. NOT AGAIN!

THE PLANE SPEEDS DOWN THE TRACK, LIFTS UP, AND—ALMOST AT ONCE—SLAMS INTO THE SAND ON ITS LEFT WING.

KLUNK

THE CROWD SIGHS. WILBUR HAS POINTED THE PLANE UP AT TOO STEEP AN ANGLE TOO SOON.

IT TAKES THE BROTHERS TWO DAYS TO REPAIR THE FLYER. DECEMBER 17: A COLD BLUSTERY DAY WITH WIND RIPPING AT MORE THAN 20 MILES PER HOUR.

IT'S FREEZING AND BLOWING OUT HERE. DO WE OR DON'T WE?

WILBUR AND ORVILLE WONDER WHETHER TO ATTEMPT THE FLIGHT AGAIN.

I SAY YES.

AND I AGREE. BECAUSE I WANT TO GET HOME FOR CHRISTMAS.

COME ON.

ONCE MORE THEY SUMMON THE HELPERS, AND THE GROUP HAULS THE PLANE TO THE HILLTOP.

TODAY IT'S ORVILLE'S TURN.

THE BROTHERS PAUSE FOR A BRIEF MOMENT AND SHAKE HANDS.

IS THIS IT—AT LONG LAST?

NOW! INTO THE AIR!

ORVILLE STARTS THE MOTOR AS WILBUR HOLDS UP ONE WING AT ITS TIP TO BALANCE THE FLYER.

THE MACHINE STARTS ROLLING DOWNHILL. WILBUR, STILL GRIPPING THE WING, RUNS ALONGSIDE. DOWN, DOWN, DOWN.

WILBUR LETS GO.

THAT AFTERNOON, THE WRIGHTS WALK INTO TOWN AND SEND A TELEGRAM. THEIR FATHER HAS GIVEN THEM A DOLLAR TO WIRE HOME, WHERE HE AND KATHARINE ANXIOUSLY AWAIT THE NEWS—

—WHICH ARRIVES WITH A FEW SLIGHT MISTAKES, INCLUDING THE INCORRECT TIME THE FLYER STAYED IN THE AIR.

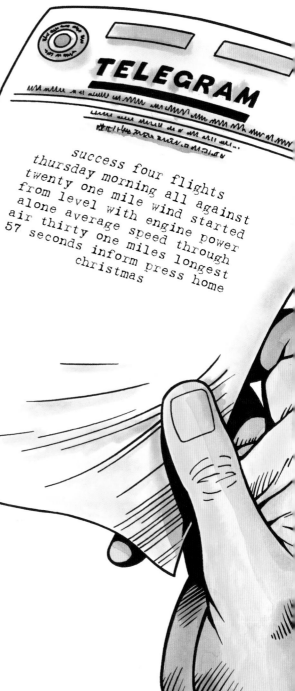

TELEGRAM

success four flights thursday morning all against twenty one mile wind started from level with engine power alone average speed through air thirty one miles longest 57 seconds inform press home christmas

AFTERWORD

THE WRIGHT BROTHERS' STORY DID NOT END AT KITTY HAWK. AS THE BROTHERS WELL KNEW, THERE WAS MORE WORK TO BE DONE ON THE AIRPLANE. SOME OF THE PROBLEMS STILL TO BE RESOLVED INCLUDED MAKING THE TAKEOFF SIMPLER, LEARNING TO EXECUTE COMPLETE TURNS IN THE AIR, AND DESIGNING THE PLANE SO THAT THE PILOT COULD FLY SITTING UP. IN 1904 AND 1905, THE BROTHERS USED AN EMPTY PASTURE NEAR THEIR HOME IN DAYTON FOR MANY ADDITIONAL EXPERIMENTS AND TESTS.

MEANWHILE, ONLY SLOWLY DID PEOPLE IN THE UNITED STATES AND ABROAD BECOME AWARE OF THE WRIGHT BROTHERS AND THE IMPORTANCE OF THEIR INVENTION. FOR SEVERAL YEARS, THE AMERICAN GOVERNMENT SHOWED NO INTEREST IN THE WRIGHTS' FLYING MACHINE. FINALLY, IN 1908, THE BROTHERS WERE ABLE TO CONVINCE THE GOVERNMENT THAT FLIGHT WAS POSSIBLE AND USEFUL. DURING THE SAME YEAR, WILBUR WENT TO EUROPE AND GAVE A SERIES OF FLYING DEMONSTRATIONS THAT MADE HIM AND ORVILLE INSTANT CELEBRITIES.

WILBUR DIED OF AN ILLNESS IN 1912. BUT ORVILLE, WHO DIED IN 1948, LIVED TO SEE "THE AGE OF FLIGHT" EXPAND IN WAYS THAT HE AND HIS BROTHER NEVER FORESAW. TODAY THERE IS A SIXTY-FOOT-HIGH MONUMENT TO THE WRIGHT BROTHERS AT KILL DEVIL HILLS, NORTH CAROLINA. BUT PERHAPS THE REAL MONUMENTS TO THE VISION, COURAGE, AND DEDICATION OF WILBUR AND ORVILLE WRIGHT ARE THE AIRPLANES YOU SEE ABOVE YOU, FLYING BACK AND FORTH ACROSS THE COUNTRY, EVERY DAY.

ROBERT BURLEIGH HAS WRITTEN MANY BOOKS FOR CHILDREN, INCLUDING *FLIGHT: THE JOURNEY OF CHARLES LINDBERGH*, ILLUSTRATED BY MIKE WIMMER, WHICH RECEIVED THE ORBIS PICTUS AWARD FOR NONFICTION; AND *HOOPS*, ILLUSTRATED BY STEPHEN T. JOHNSON, A *BOOKLIST* EDITORS' CHOICE AND A *SCHOOL LIBRARY JOURNAL* BEST BOOK OF THE YEAR. MR. BURLEIGH LIVES WITH HIS WIFE IN CHICAGO, ILLINOIS.

BILL WYLIE HAS ILLUSTRATED MANY COMIC BOOKS, INCLUDING THE SECRET DEFENDERS SERIES AND SINGLE ISSUES OF NOMAD, NIGHTSTALKERS, AND NAMOR, ALL PUBLISHED BY MARVEL COMICS. MR. WYLIE LIVES WITH HIS WIFE IN BROOKLYN, NEW YORK. *INTO THE AIR* IS HIS FIRST CHILDREN'S BOOK.

For Judy and Steve "Moon" Myers, with love
—R. B.

To Mom and Dad
—B. W.

www.HarcourtBooks.com

Silver Whistle is a trademark of Harcourt, Inc., registered
in the United States of America and/or other jurisdictions.

Library of Congress Cataloging-in-Publication Data
Burleigh, Robert.
Into the air: the story of the Wright brothers' first flight/
Robert Burleigh; illustrated by Bill Wylie.
p. cm.
"Silver Whistle."
1. Wright, Orville, 1871–1948—Juvenile literature.
2. Wright, Wilbur, 1867–1912—Juvenile literature. 3. Aeronautics—United States—
Biography–Juvenile literature. 4. Inventors—United States—Biography—
Juvenile literature. 5. Aeronautics—United States—History—Juvenile literature.
[1. Wright, Orville, 1871–1948. 2. Wright, Wilbur, 1867–1912.
3. Aeronautics—Biography. 4. Cartoons and comics.]
I. Wylie, Bill, ill. II. Title.
TL540.W7B87 2002
629.13'092'273—dc21 00-10857
ISBN 0-15-202492-1
ISBN 0-15-216803-6 (pb)

First edition
A C E G H F D B
A C E G H F D B (pb)

Printed in Singapore

The illustrations in this book were done in Luma dyes on card stock.
The display type and speech balloons were created by Ken Lopez.
The text type was set in WhizBang.
Color separations by Bright Arts Ltd., Hong Kong
Printed and bound by Tien Wah Press, Singapore
This book was printed on totally chlorine-free Nymolla Matte Art paper.
Production supervision by Sandra Grebenar and Pascha Gerlinger
Designed by Lydia D'moch